Live in the sunshine,

swim the sea,

drink the wild air...

Ralph Waldo Emerson

THE MAMANUCAS *fiji*

A pictorial journey through the
Mamanuca & Malolo Group of Islands, Fiji

by THREE LOOSE COCONUTS

Real action at Castaway

Relaxation at Musket Cove

FIJI'S

most popular holiday destinations include the MAMANUCA & MALOLO groups ...31 islands scattered over 2000 square kilometres of the Pacific Ocean. These islands are easily accessible from the mainland via boat, plane or helicopter - an opportunity many travellers seeking escapism have gladly taken. No visit to Fiji would be complete without seeing the stunning beauty of these islands and experiencing the warm hospitality of their people.

Come then, and take a voyage of pure MAGIC...

History

The large area often promoted to tourists as the Mamanucas actually consists of two separate groups. Contrary to widespread belief, the southern cluster of islands from Qalito (*Castaway*) to Tavarua is part of the Malolo Group. Historically, this latter group has played a far more prominent role.

In April 1794, Captain Baber reportedly sighted six islands and anchored in a bay on the west coast of Viti Levu. These islands are believed to be part of the Yasawas. It is likely he would have found the Mamanuca group too, had the ship not been attacked by natives who attempted to board!

Captain C. Bentley is credited with the discovery of Malolo in December 1799, along with several surrounding islands, probably of the Mamanuca Group.

Nothing more is recorded of these two groups until 1840, when they were visited by the United States Exploring Expedition led by US Navy Lt. Charles Wilkes. A confrontation with the natives at Malolo led to the death of two of Wilkes' men, including his own nephew.

An emotional burial service for the two men was held in the centre of Kadavu Island (*Bounty*).

Plans for retribution were swift and with coordinated attacks plus superior fire-power, the two deaths were avenged many times over.

In the aftermath of the attack, the chief promised that, while he was alive, all visitors to the island would be treated as friends and children. The old chief has long since passed on, but the tradition of warmth and friendliness extended to visitors from around the world has endured.

MAMANUCA-I-RA

VANUA LAILAI
EORI
NAVADRA
CAMEL ROCK
VANUA LEVU
KADOMO
YAVURIBA
VOMO LAILAI
VOMO

MAMANUCA GROUP

TOKORIKI
MONU
YANUYA
TAVUA
MONURIKI
NAUTANIVONO
MATAMANOA
MAMANUCA-I-CAKE

TIVUA
LAUTOKA

MANA
TAI (Beachcomber)
LEVUKA (Treasure)
KADAVU (Bounty)
VUDA POINT

NAVINI
VUNIVADRA (South Sea)

MOCIU (Honeymoon)
QALITO (Castaway)
MALOLO
WADIGI
MALAMALA (Daydream)

MALOLO LAILAI
PORT DENARAU
NADI

MALOLO GROUP

NAMOTU
TAVARUA

Vanua Levu
Yasawas
Mamanucas & Malolo
Viti Levu
Lau

FIJI ISLANDS

Kadavu

WATER, WATER...

...EVERYWHERE

WATER, WATER...

...FIND ME THERE.

Another blue day in the Mamanucas

Parasailing at Treasure

Paddling at Plantation 17

CATCH THE TRADE WINDS IN YOUR SAILS. EXPLORE. DREAM. DISCOVER."

-- Mark Twain

Boat transfers are the most popular way to get out to the islands, with regular daily circuits from several operators

Reef Heron in flight

Warm and friendly smiles are a reason why Fiji is a popular destination for visitors from around the world

Beach-raking is a daily ritual after high tide! 27

COME WEARY TRAVELLER - FEEL THE REFRESHING WARMTH OF THE SUN,
THE CALMING RHYTHM OF THE OCEAN, AS IT MEETS THE SHORE.

HEAR THE WELCOME WHISPERED IN RUSTLING PALMS OVERHEAD,
AND THE SINGING OF YOUR HEART - 'TIS WEARIED NO MORE.

Surfing Cloudbreak   *Kite-surfing Plantation*

Underwater treasures

Poolside pleasures

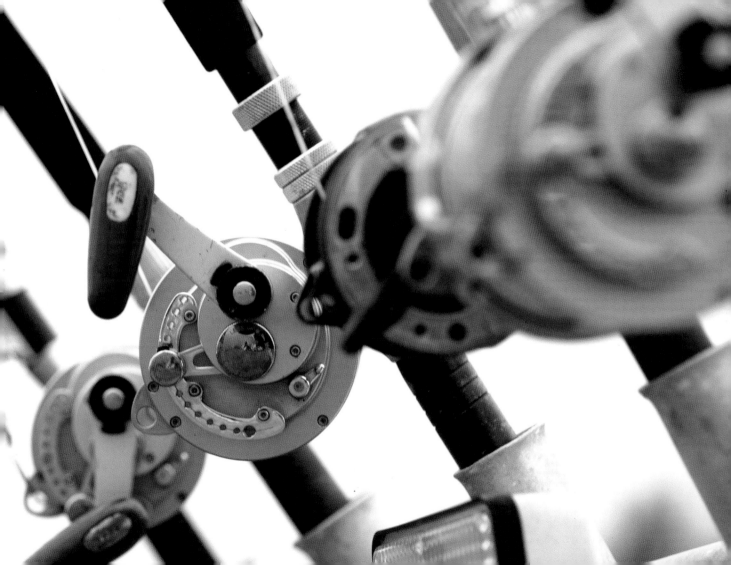

Rare Fiji Crested Iguana

Hermit crab

Starfish

Frangipani

Sand crab

Tai (Beachcomber) *from Levuka* (Treasure)

Monuriki and Monu from Matamanoa 43

44   *Qalito* (Castaway), *Mociu and Malolo from Wadigi*

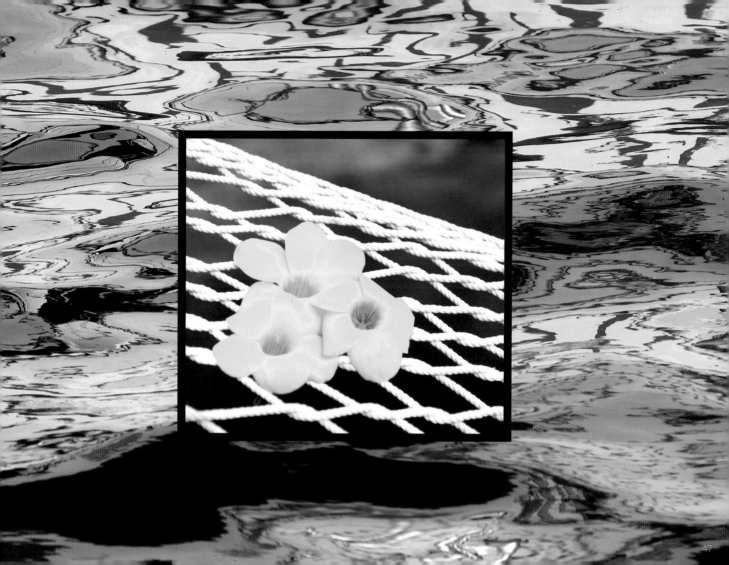

AERIAL VIEWS...

Lesser Frigate bird

Eori

Navadra

MAMANUCA-I-RA

This northernmost cluster of islands in the Mamanucas is spiritually significant to the traditional landowners of Yanuya, Malolo and Vuda.

The region is sometimes known as Narokorokoyawa, which roughly translates as "Sacred Islands". They are uninhabited and access to them is restricted.

Camel Rock

Vanua Levu

Kadomo

Yavuriba

Vomo Lailai

YAVURIBA

VOMO LAILAI

VOMO

VOMO

Yavuriba, Vomo Lailai and Vomo are largely uninhabited. The latter island is home to the Vomo Island Resort, and there are new land developments taking place on the east and south ends of the island.

Vomo

Tokoriki

MAMANUCA-I-RA

Yanuya is home to the traditional landowners of a bulk of the Mamanucas.

Tokoriki, Matamanoa and Mana have overnight resort accommodation, while Monuriki and Monu are popular day trip destinations.

Tavua and Tokoriki are currently undergoing resort and land development.

TOKORIKI

YANUYA

MONU

MONURIKI

TAVUA

MATAMANOA

NAUTANIVONO

MANA

Yanuya

Monu

Tavua

Nautanivono

Matamanoa

Mana

THE ISLETS

The sandy coral islands of the Mamanucas are popular tourist destinations. Those wanting a quick island experience can take advantage of the day trips available to most of the region.

The islands' size makes them easy to walk around – an opportunity most visitors will seize. There's something curiously satisfying about returning to the starting point without having to retrace your steps!

TIVUA

N

TAI ●
(*Beachcomber*)   LEVUKA
(*Treasure*)

KADAVU
(*Bounty*)

VUNIVADRA
(*South Sea*)

● NAVINI

MALAMALA
(*Daydream*)

Levuka (TREASURE)

Tai (beachcomber) 67

Kadavu (BOUNTY)

Navini

Vunivadra (SOUTH SEA)

Malamala (DAYDREAM)

MALOLO GROUP

Qalito (*Castaway*) is where it all began in 1966, when Dick Smith opened Fiji's first island resort.

Others quickly followed and now, forty years on, this group of islands remains a favourite destination for day trippers and tropical holiday seekers alike.

Mociu (HONEYMOON)

Qalito (CASTAWAY)

Wadigi

Malolo Lailai

Malolo Lailai

Namotu

Tavarua

NI SA MOCE

DESIGN
PHOTOGRAPHY
PUBLISHING

Three Loose Coconuts.

PRINTING

Printed in China through
Colorcraft Ltd, Hong Kong.

Printed in July 2006.

CIP

USP Library Cataloguing-in-Publication data:

Mamanuca's: Fiji.

ISBN 0 9587563 9 2

1. Resorts - Fiji - Pictorial works.
2. Fiji - Pictorial works.
3. Fiji - Description and travel.

80 p.: ill.; 21 x 15   919.611

VINAKA

As ever, thanks must go to *Ratu Yalo Vuku* Paul Geraghty for his invaluable advice and assistance in obtaining research material on the Mamanucas. Dick Watling, Josie at Musket Cove, Ian at Island Hoppers, Errol at Nadi Bay, and Joe Casey for the tea.

OTHER BOOKS *by the Nuts...*

FIJI TIME

UNFORGETTABLE
A Coconut Cookbook

UNDER THE MANGO TREE
A Nadi Bay Cookbook

PETER   ROB   GLENBO

THREE LOOSE COCONUTS:

PO Box 1131
Coolangatta 4225 Australia

Phone + 61 7 5536 3330
Fax + 61 7 5536 1900

info@threeloosecoconuts.com

www.threeloosecoconuts.com

REFERENCES

Derrick, R.A. 1951,
The Fiji Islands. A Geographical Handbook,
Government Printing Press, Suva.

Derrick, R.A. 2001, *History of Fiji*,
Government Printing Press, Suva.

Wilkes, Charles. 1985, *United States Exploring Expedition Volume 3*, Fiji Museum, Suva.